Free from Fear
WOMEN IN EL SALVADOR'S CHURCH

Free from Fear
WOMEN IN EL SALVADOR'S CHURCH

Pamela Hussey

Preface by Jon Sobrino

First published 1989
Catholic Institute for International Relations (CIIR)
22 Coleman Fields, London N1 7AF, England

© Pamela Hussey 1989

British Library Cataloguing in Publication Data

Hussey, Pamela
    Free From Fear
    1. El Salvador. Christian communities. Role of women.
    I. Title
    267'. 097284

ISBN 1 85287 026 5

Printed in England by the Russell Press Ltd,
Bertrand Russell House, Gamble Street, Nottingham NG7 4ET

CONTENTS

Acknowledgments vii

Preface ix

Map of El Salvador *facing page* 1

Introduction 1

1 The Context 3

2 The Challenge 9

3 The Response 17

4 Signs of Liberation 33

5 Signs of Hope 43

Conclusion 57

Acknowledgements

This book would never have been written without the generous help and cooperation of many people. I owe a debt of gratitude to Sister Anselma of the Sisters of St Clare, who organised my visits in the country and whose wisdom and judgement I found invaluable; to the St Clare communities in Gotera and San Antonio Abad for their generous hospitality and their willingness to share with me some of their experience in El Salvador. My thanks go also to the Little Community (La Pequeña Comunidad) for all I learnt from them of new ways of commitment, and to those members of the Oblates of the Heart of Jesus whom I met in the poorest and most out-of-the way places. Then there are Susan, Therese, and the countless men and women who accepted me with so much warmth wherever I went and whose courage and faith I shall never forget. My Jesuit friends Jon Sobrino, Jon Cortina and Rodolfo Cardenal of the University of Central America (UCA) gave me much useful advice and encouragement. Last but by no means least, I am grateful to my colleagues in CIIR for their support and their constructive criticism of the text. This book would have been a much poorer effort without their friendly and professional contribution.

Pamela Hussey
March 1989

Preface

Much has already been written about the Salvadorean people: stories full of suffering which inspire horror, and stories full of hope which arouse admiration. It is good, nevertheless, that the life and the death of the Salvadorean people continues to be told: their hope, poverty and faith, and their experience of oppression. This is what this book is all about.

Pamela's book is a detailed and truthful account of the death and the life of this people. It is an account written with emotion, anger, but above all gratitude. In four weeks in our country the author saw and heard so much that is sad but she also met light, creativity and dignity such as are not found elsewhere.

From El Salvador we thank Pamela for coming to our country, for the love she has shown this people, and the dedication with which she has recorded her experiences. We hope that this book will contribute to the growth of solidarity between sister countries and churches, so that we may come to know each other better and help each other more generously. We hope above all that solidarity will make us all more human, more like brothers and sisters, more like sons and daughters of the same Father.

Jon Sobrino
San Salvador
March 1989

Introduction

The Latin American bishops, meeting at Puebla, Mexico, in 1979, identified some of the 'most significant and renewal-oriented tendencies that the Spirit is promoting in the church' (Puebla Conclusions 723). One of these tendencies was the preferential option for the poor, another was integration into the life of the local church.

> Pastoral openness in one's labours and a preferential option for the poor represent the most notable tendency of religious life in Latin America (Puebla 733).
>
> One notices a rediscovery and a conscious experience of the mystery of the local church, as well as a growing desire to participate and to contribute the riches of one's own vocational charism (Puebla 736).

This book, published ten years after the Puebla Conference, is the account of my four-week visit to El Salvador in February 1988, when I saw the preferential option for the poor and the integration into the life of the local church being lived by the sisters and by the Christian communities with which they are so intimately involved. In a sense, I had already been drawn into the lives of the people of El Salvador through my work over the previous eight years on CIIR's Latin America desk. This contact has not only renewed my own life as a religious, but has also given me a vision of a new way of being the church and a renewed understanding of Christian commitment which I believe has much to say to us in Europe. This growing conviction was the inspiration for my journey.

My purpose in going to El Salvador had been to meet women religious living and working among the poorest and most marginalised sectors of the population, and to report on their work and on the effect this involvement had had on the way they understand and live their religious consecration. I soon found, however, that by virtue of this very involvement I could scarcely separate sisters and people — the relationship between them was too close and too vital. So my book is about all those I met, especially the women, and how they are participating in the process of liberation, how, in Christian terms, they are proclaiming the kingdom of life in defiance of an oppressive, death-dealing order.

Visitors to El Salvador are struck by the fact that the new society is already being built. A liberation theology is the expression in theological language of what is already happening, of a liberation from personal sin and from structures of sin which is already taking place.

> Theology has need of 'theological occurrences' in the present — historical realities that are God's word and God's people's word. Without these current events, theology will be reduced to a commentary on realities of the past — and so, at times, to texts of the past. All genuine theology lives on the manifestation of God in the present and on the response of God's people in faith, hope and love in the present (Jon Sobrino, Foreword to *Faith of a People*, New York, Orbis, and London, CIIR, 1986, p.xv).

The title *Free from Fear* is intended as a tribute to all those men and women, young and old, Christian or not, whose commitment to the cause of the poor has been stronger than their fear of arrest, torture and death.

> No blow is mortal where there is
> no fear of death.

1
The Context

I left for El Salvador on Friday 5 February 1988 on a Virgin Atlantic flight from Gatwick to Miami. It was Comic Relief day and the cabin crew wore red noses and collected over £500 from us on the flight. There being no connecting service, I spent a night in Miami, then took an Eastern Airways flight to San Salvador, arriving early in the afternoon. My four-week visit had begun. I had arranged to spend my first week with the Sisters of St Clare in Gotera, in the Department of Morazán, and two of the community, Anselma and Anne, met me at the airport. It was hard to believe, as we drove into the capital in the afternoon sun, with the Pacific glinting on our left, that the violence which had cost thousands of innocent civilian lives, including those of the four US churchwomen raped and murdered somewhere not far from this very road, was claiming ever more victims.

At the hotel, as we sipped cold drinks by the swimming pool and later ate an excellent supper, I realised that it is possible to live in El Salvador as if poverty, repression and war did not exist. If you keep to the hotels, the expensive shopping centres and the wealthy residential districts, you can almost forget the terrible reality. Sadly, as I later saw, even Christians — priests and sisters among them — can so withdraw into their own secure capsule that the real world may go unheeded.

That first evening, in those comfortable and relaxed surroundings, I heard of the new technique of killing by injection of poison then in use by the security forces. No marks of torture are left on the body to be photographed and denounced — the victim is dumped and slowly decomposes.

Pope John Paul II, in his encyclical *Sollicitudo Rei Socialis* (December 1987) speaks of 'the widening of the gap between the areas of the so-called North and the developing South'. He goes on:

> This geographical terminology is only indicative, since one cannot ignore the fact that the frontiers of wealth and poverty intersect within the societies themselves, whether developed or developing. In fact, just as social inequalities down to the level of poverty exist in rich countries, so, in parallel fashion, in the less developed countries one often sees manifestations of selfishness and a flaunting of wealth which is as disconcerting as it is scandalous (14).

What is particularly scandalous in El Salvador is that the interests and privilege of the rich minority are being defended against the legitimate demands of the poor majority, and that, whatever the professed intentions of the United States government, billions of dollars have been poured into El Salvador in support of this struggle of a tiny elite to preserve its economic and social domination over the people.

The sisters I met are in touch with the marginalised and oppressed communities which make up this majority, and through them I came into contact with some of the 600,000 Salvadoreans displaced by the war, with some of the 4,500 refugees (out of a total refugee population of 500,000) who returned from the Mesa Grande camp in Honduras in October 1987, with victims of the 1986 earthquake still living in makeshift shacks, with basic ecclesial communities, catechists, health promoters — a whole range of people trying to cope with the results of poverty and war and committed to building a new society. They ask only to be allowed to live as human beings, with a roof over their heads, enough food, education and health care, and some participation in the task of building up their country.

The war
El Salvador is a small country about the size of Wales, in which the majority has always been poor (65% of the rural population is landless; 2% own 60% of the land) and now has to bear the brunt of the civil war in addition to the poverty and repression which have been their lot since the Spanish conquest.

The war has been raging since 1980 between government forces who, despite their lip-service to democracy, are protecting the interests of the small, wealthy elite, and an alliance of guerrilla groups which emerged in the 1970s out of popular organisations, the Farabundo Martí Front for National Liberation (FMLN). It was Farabundo Martí who planned the short-lived 1932 insurrection, which cost the lives of no more than 30 people and resulted in the massacre of between 20,000 and 30,000 peasants in the ensuing reprisals.

> This massacre has become a potent symbol in contemporary Salvadorean politics. The oligarchy believe that similar tactics today would secure their power for another generation (*Comment: El Salvador*, CIIR 1988).

The role of the United States in this war is decisive and dreadful. Since 1980 it has given more than three billion dollars to El Salvador in economic and military aid, it has equipped the Salvadorean armed forces and trained more than 19,000 officers and men. Since 1983 it has controlled the Salvadorean government's military strategy.

Apart from those killed in combat, well over 40,000 non-combatant civilians have been murdered by death squads and security forces since October 1979. 40,000 is a conservative estimate, including only fully documented cases.

Religion
Salvadoreans have been Christian since colonial times — religion for them has never been marginal but always a part of life. But, as a Salvadorean sister said, 'Religion can serve to put people to sleep as well as to wake them up,' and in El Salvador, as in other parts of Latin America, religion was often used to keep people passive and resigned to their poverty.

Historically the Latin American church has been allied with the wealthy and middle classes, the powerful land-owners and the rich industrial and commercial sector. It has enjoyed a privileged position as the upholder of the status quo — a position which has often led to its giving legitimacy to oppressive régimes. Much was made of St Paul's exhortation to the Romans to 'be subject to the authorities governing us. He who ... resists authority goes against the order established by God, and those who resist deserve to be condemned' (Rom 13:2). Acceptance of the established order was a popular theme for Sunday sermons, regardless of whether that order was itself an offence to God. A peasant remembers how it used to be:

> Dear children — the priest used to say, and I remember it — never want what others have, because that is bad. Because covetousness is evil, dear children. He who covets will not be saved. You must be content with what God gives. Because God knows who he wants to give to, and who he does not want to give to. ... If you are drunkards, if you gamble when you are poor, what would you be, dear children, if you had money?' (*Don Lito de El Salvador*, by María López Vigil, San Salvador, UCA Editores, 1987).

The Second Vatican Council proposed a new model of church: more community than institution or pyramid of power, more concerned with people than with preserving its own life and structures; a church that makes its own the joys and hopes, the griefs and anxieties of all people, especially of those who are poor or afflicted in any way (see the Council's Constitution on the Church in the Modern World [*Gaudium et Spes*], 1).

At two important Conferences of the Latin American bishops, at Medellín, Colombia, in 1968, and Puebla, Mexico, in 1979, the bishops, in response to the demands for justice coming up from the continent's poor, and in fidelity to the vision of Vatican II, turned to the poor majority:

> The Latin American bishops cannot remain indifferent in the face of the tremendous social injustices existent in Latin America, which keep the majority of our peoples in dismal poverty, which in many cases becomes inhuman wretchedness.
>
> A deafening cry pours from the throats of millions, asking their pastors for a liberation that reaches them from nowhere else (Medellín, Conclusions, 14.2).

The church began a process of change at Medellín and ranged itself with the poor against the forces of domination. The alliance with the poor was reaffirmed at Puebla in 1979, and the now famous 'preferential option for the poor' was confirmed, though not without resistance from some sections of the hierarchy, who did not like the direction taken at Medellín. The Latin American church embraced a three-fold task: denunciation of the sinfulness of the world, including 'sinful structures' in society, annunciation of the good news of the kingdom of justice, love and peace, and a solemn commitment to build this kingdom in partnership with the poor.

After Medellín the Central American bishops met at Antigua, Guatemala, in 1970, and produced their own document, addressing themselves specifically to the poor. Later that year the Salvadorean bishops' conference organised a pastoral week to reflect on the Antigua declaration. At this meeting Salvadorean society and the church's place in it were scrutinised, and conclusions for future ministry were set out in a final document. Those attending the meeting recognised that discrimination, institutionalised in a system which was justified and defended to the point where the human and Christian development of the people was stunted, was built into the fabric of Salvadorean society. Two ecclesial models were presented: the first that of a self-satisfied church, averse to questioning and change, interested mainly in increasing the number of sacraments dispensed, a church anxious to preserve its alliance with the dominant class and therefore afraid to speak out against injustice lest it lose its privileges or suffer persecution. The second model was that of a church in a constant process of conversion seeking to become incarnate in Salvadorean society as it really was, that is, mostly poor.

Unfortunately, the Salvadorean bishops were not ready for such a radical analysis and the conclusions which followed from it. Although the bishops' conference of El Salvador (CEDES) had called the meeting, only two bishops, Mgr Gregorio Rosa Chávez and Mgr Arturo Rivera Damas, were present throughout, and subsequently the conference as a whole rejected many of the meeting's conclusions, publishing their own watered-down version of the final document (see Rodolfo Cardenal, *Historia de una esperanza. Vida de Rutilio Grande*, San Salvador, UCA Editores, 1985).

These divisions, which reflect those in the Latin American church as a whole, are not, it must be noted, the traditional ones between hierarchy and clergy on the one side, and the laity on the other. They cut right across the structures. They divide those who are committed to the people of God (a Vatican II term which in Latin America becomes 'the people of God's poor') and to the historical efficacy of Christian love, leading to a commitment to the transformation of unjust social and economic systems, from those who for a variety of reasons (fear of losing a privileged position, fear of persecution) fail to take up a clear position, but who, despite their declarations of 'impartiality', in fact favour the interests of the landowning and business élite whose patronage they have so long enjoyed. These differences of viewpoint cannot be equated with the European divide between so-called 'conservatives' and 'progressives'. They mark, rather, a tension between a commitment to social change seen as a demand of the gospel, and a model of church which emphasises 'spirituality' and asks no questions about repressive structures.

The angry resistance of the landowners and industrialists to any movement of the church in favour of social change was seen recently when the Salvadorean Association of Coffee-growers (ASCAFE) published an open letter, dated 7 July 1988, to the President of the Bishops' Conference, Mgr Marco René Revelo, criticising Archbishop Rivera Damas's call for a national debate on peace. ASCAFE thought this initiative was tantamount to 'imposing marxism on our country through the so-called theology of liberation' and reminded members of the Bishops' Conference that 'it is not the church's task to promote the change of structures but to procure conversion based on the supernatural dimension of the person'.

2
The Challenge

Forces of evil
On my first Sunday in El Salvador, at mass in the cathedral, I heard Bishop Gregorio Rosa Chávez, the auxiliary bishop of San Salvador, denounce the violence of the previous week in a now famous homily, reminiscent of the Sunday homilies of Archbishop Romero.

Tutela Legal, the archdiocesan legal aid office, had reported twenty-six violent killings in that week, and the bishop referred particularly to the killing by soldiers of the First Artillery Brigade of two peasants and a boy from San José Guayabal: 'What a stupid way to make the country people feel that their well-being and security are being looked after!'

Commenting on the gospel account of Jesus casting out demons (Mk 1:29-39), the bishop said, 'The works of the devil are obvious in private life and in the way society is organised. ... The hand of the devil is also present in those who play so cynically with human life, coldly murdering their neighbour or making a fat profit out of war.'

Indeed, after a week in El Salvador I was saying to myself, 'What is happening in this country is diabolic.' St Paul's words to the Ephesians came alive: 'Our battle is not against human forces but against the rulers and authorities and their dark powers that govern this world. We are struggling against the spirits and supernatural forces of evil' (Eph. 6:12). As Pope John Paul remarks in *Sollicitudo Rei Socialis*, 'One cannot easily gain a profound understanding of the reality that confronts us unless we give a name to the root of the evils which afflict us'(36). Evil is tangible in El Salvador: it is structured and organised, a terrible machine which upholds the power of the few and exploits the many, countering by brutal repression their legitimate demands for a decent human life.

The following Sunday Father Jesús Delgado, director of the archdiocesan weekly newspaper, *Orientación,* preached a homily in the cathedral. Fr Delgado referred first to the criticism of Bishop Rosa Chávez for the previous Sunday's denunciation. He remarked on the fact that the controversy had centred on the denunciation itself, and not on the events which it denounced.

> Not a word of horror at such cruel killings; not a word of compassion for the families concerned; not a word of indignation at the increase in repression. All this shows the tragic situation in which the armed forces and the government have once again focused on the form and not the content, on the words of a bishop — that they do not like — and not on the blood of the murdered. Yet another proof that there is no concern for truth, only for propaganda.

Astonishingly, however, Fr Delgado ended his homily with these words:

> Believe me, I say this with profound conviction. The two solid institutions in this country on which the destiny and the future of the country rest, as they have done until the present day, are the church and the armed forces. ... Since the independence of this country, the church with its priests and the armed forces with their troops have been, are, and will continue to be the solid bases on which rest freedom, unity and our faith in God.

The fortnightly *Letter to the Churches* published by the Central American University commented:

> These words are incredible. Archbishop Romero clearly stated that if any social group was the companion and natural partner of the church, it was the people, the unimportant ones in history, and not any institution with power, far less the one with the military power which has been used in so macabre a way against the people.

Fr Delgado's homily was an example of the ambiguous reactions of some church leaders to what is happening in the country. To those who have been inspired by the homilies of Archbishop

Romero, such sentiments are a betrayal of a church that has made the poor its first concern and priority.

Workers' protest

After the mass that Sunday students distributed leaflets advertising a march to celebrate the second anniversary of the formation of the UNTS, the National Union of Salvadorean Workers. 'Experience has taught oppressed and exploited peoples, and especially the Salvadorean people,' the leaflet began, 'that only by uniting can they defeat the enemy who exploits, deceives and murders them in cold blood.'

On the way to the bus station for the four-hour journey to Gotera next day, Anne and I passed the UNTS demonstration and marvelled at the courage of those who had come out on the streets with their banners and their slogans, especially the intrepid Mothers of the Disappeared, clearly recognisable by their white headscarves. A small political space has opened since the five Central American presidents signed the Guatemala Peace Agreement on 7 August 1987, but the possibility of army and/or police intervention at gatherings of this kind is ever-present.

I was to see for myself on many occasions how, by uniting and organising, the Salvadorean peasants and workers have gained strength to confront the powerful forces that try to silence their just demands, and how the powerful fear and seek to destroy this unity and organisation.

Morazán

The four-hour bus journey to Gotera took us through beautiful country, brown since it was the dry season, but splashed with green here and there near a river, and dominated by the peaks of the San Vicente and San Miguel volcanoes. The beauty could not altogether hide the harsh reality: we passed hillsides burnt black by the army in its efforts to destroy the crops which are the people's source of food. The result is that Morazán has become a desert over the years; the water table has been lowered by 70%, the rivers are dried up, and the soil is so poor that the peasants are obliged to plant high up on very steep slopes.

At all the stops the bus was besieged by women selling tortillas (rather tough thick pancakes made of ground maize and water and cooked over an open fire), meat on skewers, small cakes, mangoes and other fruit, and *frescos* — fruit drinks in plastic bags. You either drink through a straw or suck through a hole bitten in the plastic (with disastrous results for the unskilled). The food was carefully presented in small paper serviettes and the *frescos* were well iced. Salvadoreans believe in selling you something for your money — not once in my stay did I encounter a beggar. On the bus and throughout my visit I was impressed by the clean and tidy appearance of the women and the trouble they took with the little they had to make the most of their appearance.

As we went on, more and more people crowded into the bus and eventually onto the roof; every seat was taken inside and the aisle was jammed with people carrying hens, fruit and vegetables to market.

The army was very visible all along the route — the Panamerican highway — especially at bridges, which were preceded by ramps and had sentry posts at both ends. The buses are stopped at check points along the way when soldiers inspect people's identity cards. We were only stopped once. Anselma, travelling the day before, had been stopped three times. Women line up in the shade of the bus, men behind. The whole thing takes place very quietly but the tension can be felt: out of date papers or evidence that you come from a 'subversive' zone can mean serious trouble. It is at such times, too, that men are forcibly recruited into the army. A 'press gang' method of recruitment is used: young men and boys are literally grabbed off the streets, outside schools, places of work, off buses. These lightning strikes were then taking place regularly, about once a month, and more often if the army had suffered heavy losses. The sons of the wealthy have ways of eluding conscription, so the soldiers come mostly from the peasant and working classes.

We arrived in Gotera in the middle of the afternoon and recovered over a salad tea. It was much hotter here than in the capital but the house was cool and airy. A dining area and open veranda look onto a central courtyard fresh with greenery; the chapel is on the opposite side of the courtyard, and the bedrooms and showers form the other two sides. Immediately inside the front door are two spacious rooms where the numerous callers are received and looked after, given a meal, or beds for the night.

Morazán is one of the departments or provinces which has been hardest hit by the war. A sister told me that it is known as 'the department of fear and death' and that she had been very afraid of going there — 'but I got on the bus and came'. Her fear was overcome by the strong call she felt to be with her people. Gotera is a small, rural and very poor town, and the parish is extensive, covering ten towns, each with its cluster of sub-districts, totalling seventy or eighty communities.

Displaced people began pouring into Gotera from the war zone in 1979 and the population of 5,000 has been swollen by 14,000 refugees and an army garrison of 3,000. A great many people have, however, remained in the zone controlled by the FMLN in the north of the department, beyond the Torola river. (The so-called 'controlled zones' are those areas where there is no state administrative structure or fixed military presence; here political and military organisation are under the control of the FMLN).

Taking sides with the poor

An important sector of the Salvadorean church — important by virtue of its commitment and dynamism rather than its numbers — has responded to the appeal of the bishops at Puebla for 'conversion on the part of the whole church to a preferential option for the poor'.

Many priests and sisters began to forge links with the poorest, 'accompanying' them, as they put it — moving into the most marginalised sectors where the misery, oppression and injustice are clearly seen. This response to what Jon Sobrino has called 'the inescapable necessity of incarnation in the Central American reality' has transformed the way they see their religious consecration and ministry. To quote Jon Sobrino again,

> This incarnation put Christians and religious in a more or less immediate contact with the real poor, and they became the 'locus' of the Christian life. ... The important thing about the option for the poor is that Christian life was understood as *a practice of service* to the poor, which became increasingly seen as a practice learned from and carried out among the poor (*Spirituality of Liberation*, New York, Orbis Books, 1988, p. 3, translation adapted).

In the early 1970s the then Archbishop of San Salvador, Mgr Luis Chávez, became aware, through his pastoral visits to rural areas, of the extreme poverty of the people, whom he found abandoned by both state and church. He asked the women's congregations to organise, in their holidays, ten- to fifteen-day visits to these rural areas, to take the people the good news of the kingdom. This 'insertion into reality' was to have a profound effect both on the congregations themselves and on the Salvadorean church. It led to the setting-up of a permanent group of sisters from different congregations whose aim was to cooperate in the pastoral work of walking and working with the people in their process of liberation, building with them a new world where justice, love and peace would reign. To quote from a report of the Conference of Religious of El Salvador (CONFRES), these sisters 'give a clear witness of poverty, know how to adjust to a low budget so that they can evangelise from a humble dwelling, having as their centre the eucharistic Jesus and the brother and sister in need of bread'. It is sad to record that its support for this group earned for CONFRES the label 'communist' from some congregations, who then withdrew from the conference.

In the archdiocese of San Salvador all but one of the fifteen women's congregations have sisters in pastoral work, totalling twenty-six communities or small groups in all. In the rest of the country there are sisters working in fourteen parishes.

The Sisters of St Clare

Anselma went to El Salvador in 1972, the first member of her congregation to work in the third world. The Poor Clares, the second Franciscan Order founded by St Francis and St Clare in 1253, had convents in Ireland very early in their history, but with the coming of the Reformation these convents were closed and the Sisters dispersed. Some left Ireland to seek refuge on the Continent. In 1629 some Irish Poor Clares returned to their native land from a convent in the Netherlands. For almost 200 years they suffered persecution and were obliged to flee from one place to another, but remained steadfast in their resolve to continue their life of cloistered contemplation. Their active apostolate began in 1804, when their situation became so difficult that they were obliged to take on the work of looking after orphans, which led them into educational work. Since the Second Vatican Council (1962-65) the congregation has grown, with new foundations in England, Scotland, Wales and the United States. Its history of persecution, poverty and insecurity is a fitting precedent for the sisters' present ministry in El Salvador. In keeping with their long tradition of solidarity with the poor, they established a convent in El Salvador in 1972.

In the early 1970s the pastoral team in Gotera consisted of two sisters and three or four Irish Franciscan priests. Throughout this decade the Salvadorean government's response to the legitimate demands for recognition of their rights by peasant federations, urban trade unions, shanty town dwellers, students, Christian groups and reformist politicians was repression, which increased in intensity throughout the decade and reached a peak in the early 1980s. By 1980 the team's pastoral work had to stop and the diocesan centre for catechists had to be closed. Two catechists had been killed, others had felt in the light of their Christian commitment that there was no other option but to take up arms for the people, and left to join the guerrillas in the mountains. Still others left for the mountains to continue there their pastoral work, which, interestingly, they found they could do with more freedom than in the rest of the country, where permits and passes were required by the state and military authorities.

From 1981 to 1984 the work in Gotera was reduced by the war to simple assistance, giving out food, clothes, medical supplies, even though this apparently ran counter to the original aim of helping the people to help themselves and thus retain a measure of self-respect and independence.

By 1985 the attacks on the church seemed to have diminished, though they did not cease entirely, and meetings for catechists began again and are now held openly in five different centres. Paradoxically, however, the repression has again intensified since the signing by the Central American heads of state of the Guatemala Peace Agreement in August 1987, and many people told me that the situation was as bad as it had been in the early 1980s.

The sisters received more reports of human rights abuses in the first six months of 1988 than in the previous three years. In El Salvador as in Guatemala, 'the extreme right wing in the armed forces and the business community have reacted to the possibility of dialogue with the guerrillas by stepping up repression against the local opposition' (*Comment*: *The Central American Peace Process*, CIIR 1988).

Evangelisation

There are now thirteen Sisters of St Clare in El Salvador, eight of them young Salvadoreans, and a second house has been opened in San Antonio Abad, a poor neighbourhood in the capital. The Franciscan priests also now include Salvadoreans in their number. Since the early 1980s nurses of the Mennonite Central Committee in the United States have formed part of the parish team.

Seven groups have been set up in the Gotera parish for catechesis, literacy, health, justice and peace, youth, the family, and one dealing with training sessions for the pastoral team.

In the early days the sisters used to go to the barracks to complain about human rights abuses and enquire about people who had been detained, but their persistent denunciations and their active concern for the victims and their families have earned them the labels 'communist' and 'subversive'. The sisters now have a close relationship with the Red Cross officials who have set up an office in Gotera. Recently, during what had been announced by the army as a distribution of food, clothing and medicine, a crowd was made to listen to the local Colonel denounce the Catholic parish of Gotera, the Catholic church in general, the International Red Cross and other human rights agencies. The Colonel claimed that the priests and sisters were guerrillas. The people were warned to stay away from them and from the other organisations. The handout of old clothes and medicines was simply a pretext for the denunciation.

The pastoral team's method of functioning has adapted over the years to the changing situation in the country: they now concentrate on building Christian communities, training leaders and helping people to reflect on their lives in the light of God's word in the bible. 'My aim now,' says Anselma, 'is, above all, to be with the people, to support them and love them. Fifteen years ago the aim would have been very different — more on the lines of doing things for rather than being with.' The team felt called and challenged by the poor and their powerlessness to abandon old and now inappropriate forms of ministry and to move into new ways of evangelising, based upon a liberating presence among the people.

3
The Response

Preparation for a life of service: redefining vocation
In 1986 the Latin American Conference of Religious (CLAR) published the results of a survey showing that the number of those joining religious congregations from the wealthy and upper middle classes had diminished to 6.05%, while those joining from the rural and urban working classes had risen to over 52%.

Many of the sisters I spoke to came from peasant families and had previously been involved with the church as catechists. They had found that life in a religious community offered the possibility of a more total commitment to the service of the people. 'Our big commitment is to the people,' said one sister, 'and the congregation gives us more freedom to develop and to give the little that we have.' They know that they receive more than they give: they see themselves as coming from and belonging to the people, the strength of whose faith, hope and love sustains and confirms them in their own commitment.

> We haven't come to give the people anything — we have nothing to give. We have come to learn from them, from their rich spirituality, based on their experience. The people give us courage to go on. Their faith and hope have deepened with suffering. They know that God is always with them, whereas we sometimes get disheartened with difficulties and forget that God is present.

Of the thirteen Sisters of St Clare at present in El Salvador, eight are Salvadoreans aged between 20 and 40. Four have already made their first vows in the congregation; four are still in training. Screening is very tight, owing to the particular circumstances, and the various training stages, up to first profession of vows, total about six years.

Those joining the congregation share with the sisters the responsibilities of pastoral work complicated by the problems brought by the war: the displacement of large numbers of people because of the aerial bombardment and the destruction of homes and crops; captures, disappearances, torture, killings, and a whole range of other abuses of human rights. Daily confrontation with these problems requires maturity, initiative, compassion and discretion, and the long training period is geared to discovering whether the candidate has the potential for this demanding and sometimes dangerous ministry. Good will is not enough in the present situation — if it ever is — and commitment to the service of the people has to be matched by a greater maturity and a more developed judgment than is sometimes required elsewhere from a candidate for the religious life.

Anselma commented:

> Formation is for life — and a life being lived in a specific historical, geographical, social and political reality. We do not live in a vacuum. Certain values will of course be universal, but the means of expressing them will be totally different. Can the vow of poverty mean the same thing in a welfare state and in a country where some are literally dying of malnutrition? Is 'saying the office' enough when you have with you in the chapel a family whose father has just been tortured or murdered? Is it good enough to give food to the people who come to the door when you know that injustice, greed and unequal distribution of wealth are causing incredible hardship to millions of people? At our peril would we try to impose a ready-made formation on the young people of Latin America today, who really desire with all their hearts to 'bring the Good News to the poor', and to share in the mission of Jesus.

The vows take on a special meaning when service of the people is at the heart of the commitment. Obedience can mean hearing the will of God in, for example, the advice of a peasant not to go to a certain place because it is dangerous, and changing plan accordingly. 'Poverty,' said a sister, 'does not mean lacking everything, but being ready to have or not to have. It means not having anything securely, sharing the insecurity of the poor.' (This sister later had her truck, on which she depended for her visits to refugee camps, taken from her by armed men.) 'Our consecration to the Lord doesn't mean flight from the world — I don't think flight is fruitful. The vows have to bear fruit, to be life-giving.'

Community has to be a place of total trust: lives may depend on the discretion and sense of responsibility of the members. 'People gathered in a community,' said a sister, 'are not gathered for themselves but for others.' Their centre is not the community, but the people they serve.

Those consecrated to God in religious life have to work out their prophetic role in the church in El Salvador: how to enter into the struggle for a new society, bringing to it a Christian dimension, seeing it in terms of helping to build the Kingdom which is eternal. They must constantly reassess their option for the poor, putting aside the trappings of power and being ready to go among the people with nothing to give and a readiness to learn, open to a continual incarnation, to what Jon Sobrino has called 'living in history with spirit'.

There are no ready answers to the questions the church is facing in El Salvador today: this is a new history, and a new Word of God is being spoken, a new way of being church is developing. It requires openness, a readiness to go through a process of conversion, a willingness to 'walk humbly with our God', faith in the God of the new.

'What credibility will we have as church after the war,' asked a priest, 'if we are not now alongside the people? Can we give something to the revolution, and receive something from it, so that we build a better world together?'

Life in Gotera

Juana has recently made her vows as a Sister of St Clare, and she told me what it had been like when she first joined the community in Gotera. 'In the first days we began to answer the door to people with great problems: arrests, disappearances, people whose children or husbands had been taken. I felt the injustice of their situation and saw that the people feel defenseless: they are attacked as an ant is attacked by an elephant. So that one feels one has to contribute something and not leave the people alone, without anyone to make their voice heard.'

I spent a week in Gotera and was struck by the ordinariness of life at one level — cooking, cleaning, washing and ironing, praying — and running parallel with that, entwined with it, so to speak, the pain and the suffering of the people, the contact with terrible happenings.

The day begins at 6 a.m. with the military band playing the National Anthem (the barracks is very near the house). Then there is the sound of marching boots as the soldiers go through their drill, shouting 'Commando!' and 'We are Commandos - Commandos don't die!'. Army helicopters provide a raucous background as we pray in the chapel and then have breakfast: tea (made with tea bags — strange to see Lipton's label in El Salvador!), home-made bread (Anselma's early morning task), and marmalade. Then the people start arriving and the day begins in earnest.

Sometimes someone just wants to fill a jug with water; sometimes there is a family to be listened to, comforted, perhaps put up for the night. A man has just been released from detention and is in a state of shock; a widow has travelled miles in the hopes of finding her husband's grave, only to hear that it is too dangerous for her to visit the spot where he is buried.

One of those who came to the house while I was there was Tránsito Bonilla. He had just been released from the barracks and told us his story, obviously still very frightened. He had been stopped at an army check-point while he was carrying two hose pipes without the permit that the Army requires when goods are taken from one place to another (this makes it easier for food and building materials to be denied entrance to the camps and 'subversive' zones). He was asked if he was going to make mines with the pipes, and he said he needed them to water his plants. They let him go, but a second check-point stopped him and detained him for 'evading' the first. In the barracks he was made to do a handstand against a wall, with barbed wire just below his feet to catch them when they slipped. Then they beat him, saying he was a guerrilla, which he denied. They then put a sack of sand on his shoulders and made him do press-ups until he was near collapse. Finally, on the second day, they released him. He heard soldiers saying that two other men were going to be 'eliminated'. This incident left Tránsito very nervous and too bruised to be able to work for a week.

His story was one of many given to officials of Tutela Legal, the archdiocesan legal aid office, when they called on their monthly visit to get information about incidents in the area. A file was kept of the cases: a sad catalogue of detentions, (often accompanied by beatings), disappearances, harassment and threats, torture and death. Here are a few of the 41 incidents collected over a two-month period (of which the guerrillas were responsible for two):

> Diomedes was threatened by soldiers claiming to be guerrillas, asking him what he thought of rich people, etc. After questioning, he was beaten. The next day his brother Dionisio was detained. He was released two days later. Responsible: 4th Military Detachment.
>
> A young literacy promoter and guitar player, Emilio Baldonado Ramos, died as a result of injuries to his right leg from a landmine explosion. He was walking with five others at 6.00 p.m. to a soccer game when he decided to take a shorter path and detonated a hidden mine. He died the next morning at 3.00 from blood loss. The guerrillas in the area accepted responsibility for the mine. The guerrillas instructed the villagers again which paths were to be avoided because they were mined. [Warning the people about mines was a common practice in guerrilla-controlled territory].
>
> Oscar Arnoldo and Higinio Arrila were detained while on their way to Sociedad. They had come upon a dead body on their way. Friends thought they were detained because they found the body. Both were released the next day. Responsible: Armed soldiers.
>
> Government soldiers surrounded the homes of three women, claiming that their chicken cooperative was subversive and used solely by the guerrillas. The women, starting with only four chickens a couple of years ago, now had 60 chickens, most of which were laying. The women told the soldiers that the project was started by the church. They were told they had to have a permit and that their chicken house would be destroyed. The area was later mortared and sprayed with machine-gun fire. The women now carry a copy of the permit with them.

After studying the files the officials went off in their vehicle for further investigation. The information they collect is filed at the Tutela Legal office in the capital, a sad task for the director, María Julia Hernández.

'We are church'

Diego, Inocente and Margarito came to the house one hot morning and sat in the cool shade of the front room. Anselma assured them that I could be trusted and I went in and listened to their story. They were weather-beaten peasants, diffident, quietly spoken, poorly but cleanly dressed, their big hats clutched in their hands.

They were catechists and had been displaced from their home villages when these were totally destroyed in the aerial bombardments of the early 1980s. Now they were wanting to return and had come to discuss their plans with Anselma. After years of wandering in the mountains, going from place to place, staying in the already crowded houses of relatives or friends, many Salvadoreans are now thinking of going back to the places they left and trying to start life again. The church is supporting them in this, knowing that dependence is not good when it lasts for too long, but the risks are real and many are fearful.

Inocente told me a little about the work of the catechists in his communities and said proudly, 'Everyone takes turns leading the celebration — no one is higher than anyone else.' I saw for myself the pride with which catechists conducted the liturgy of the Word at Sunday mass, before the priest arrived to continue the celebration.

Authoritarianism in church and state, and their newly-awakened sense of their own worth and potential, and of the essential equality of all — men not being superior to women, or rich to poor — have given Salvadoreans a thirst for democratic procedures. They know that they are the church and they want their right to participate in its life and ministry to be recognised and respected.

A sister said, 'The people said they wanted us to be with them, and to tell the bishops and if possible the Pope that they wanted the living church to be with them, because they said, "We are church too. We don't think of a church of stone, of cement. If we meet under a tree, we are church."'

A ceremony of commitment

The desire for nearness to and service of the people found its full expression when two Salvadoreans, Elvia and Juana, made their vows of poverty, chastity and obedience in the church of Cacaopera, a small town north of Gotera where Juana's family lived. It was a commitment made in the midst of the people and in response to them: the whole town was involved in the preparations for the ceremony. For days groups had been cleaning the church, working on the liturgy, making small yellow and white flags inscribed with greetings: 'Glory to God on this day, Elvia and Juana', 'You too, brother (or sister), are called by the Lord'. Women were up all night making sandwich fillings in huge pots lined up along the street — among the ingredients we had taken up from Gotera the previous day I was amused to see a bottle of Lea and Perrins!

Busloads of friends and relations came out from the capital — having left at 5.00 a.m. — and stopped at our house for breakfast. It always amazed me how there was never any problem about producing food and drink, no matter how short supplies were. When we arrived in Cacaopera, the sun was blazing hot and the whole place was buzzing with anticipation of a celebration and a good time. The zone controlled by the FMLN can be seen in the middle distance — guerrillas had been into the town the day before and left leaflets.

A procession formed, song sheets were given out, and we soon moved singing along the street to the church. We were stopped at one point by two men, neither of them in their first youth, performing a complicated dance. No one minded when they went wrong and spent some time shuffling in the dust to get right again: the important thing was that they were contributing to the event.

Octavio Ortiz, a young priest who was murdered in San Antonio Abad in 1979, was a native of this town, and a picture of him was prominently displayed in the church. Elvia and Juana were now making a public commitment to follow in the steps of Octavio and the many others whose dedication to the Word and the kingdom led, as it did for the prophets and Jesus, to their death.

The two sisters sat in the front row of the congregation with the people — a man in a brightly coloured T-shirt between them — and from that symbolic position they went up to the altar to make their vows. (I remembered profession ceremonies in pre-Vatican II days witnessed only by members of the religious order concerned: no family and no representatives of the wider church.) The homily was given by a Franciscan priest, Brendan Forde, who said that he had asked the people in his Chalatenango parish what message they would like to send the sisters. Their answer had been, 'Tell them to be with us and to love us.' Brendan went on, 'Now Elvia and Juana are going to make their vows so as to be with the people, to walk with the people. You must see that they never distance themselves from you.' Turning to Elvia and Juana he said, 'You must listen to the people and listen to the Bible. And how are we going to listen to the people if we are not with them?' In this spirit the sisters added a paragraph of their own to the traditional vow formula: 'I commit myself to accompany the poor and oppressed, to seek with them in the light of the gospel the will of God and to build his kingdom of justice, love and peace according to the example of St Francis and St Clare.'

The singing was tremendously moving: asking for justice, praising God for his glory, offering their desires and their problems and their commitment.

> I hear your voice deep inside me saying
> 'Come, follow me.'
> With joy I thank you, Jesus,
> I want to say Yes!
> Knowing that you are calling me, Lord,
> I want to say Yes!
> With my brothers and in freedom,
> I want to say Yes!

At the offertory groups from each village brought up symbolic gifts: rice and beans, their daily food; books and bible, which help them to learn; and a drawing of two young men, each with a leg missing, supporting each other, a sign of fraternal love and concern.

The whole celebration lasted three hours and no one thought it too long, but we all lined up gratefully for the delicious sandwiches and *frescos* so carefully prepared for the hundreds who were there.

Under the enjoyment, the burden of suffering. Before we left, I spoke to an elderly couple who had been displaced from their town because of the bombing. Two of their sons had been killed — 'They died unjustly.' Another son and two daughters are catechists — and therefore in line for the same fate. An old woman told me how her daughter had been literally shot to pieces by soldiers as she washed in the river, leaving her small daughter to be looked after by the grandmother.

Back at the house, after waving off a busload returning to the capital, we prepared a special supper of liver casserole followed by melon and pistachio ice cream, which we ate scattered about on the veranda, enjoying the cool after the heat of the day and prolonging the mood of celebration. Celebrations are very important in El Salvador: they express a belief in the ultimate triumph of life. As Phyllis said, 'The people make a celebration out of anything. They will spend money they can ill afford on a First Communion dress, because for them this day is so special that it has to be celebrated. There are so few times in life that they can have a big celebration, that when there is one they put everything into it. They also have a whole bunch of little celebrations: if you're going away you all get together and have a *fresco*. You come back — and there's another!'

My experience in El Salvador was not only that of a people used to poverty and suffering — I was also introduced to a world where, in Gustavo Gutiérrez' words, 'being poor is a way of living, loving, praying, believing and hoping, spending leisure time...', a world which can celebrate with real joy. The world of the poor is an enrichment for the rich.

The profession ceremony at Cacaopera was the formalising of the option for the poor made by Elvia and Juana: a public commitment within the church and within the Salvadorean context, involving a definite way of life and the acceptance of risk, insecurity and danger. The option for the poor is not just a beautiful idea in El Salvador, a slogan based on desire rather than reality — it means making a real choice that transforms life. Tonia knows that the option must be more than words: 'Of course, if you read the gospel you understand what it is saying. But it is one thing to understand and another to practise. It's one thing to say "We are with the poor, we accompany them" — but it's another thing to actually take this on. I think this is very difficult. Some people have good intentions, but when it comes to assuming responsibility, that is different. Often it is a risk.'

Fear of taking a risk prevents many, including some church leaders, from assuming responsibility, from making a real option, standing with the poor and denouncing the injustices and atrocities suffered by them. But fidelity to the wind of the Spirit blowing us beyond well-known frontiers always involves risk, and those committed to this endeavour have overcome fear. Persecution, arrest, torture seem only to strengthen their resolve. A catechist, a member of an agricultural union, was detained with four others, held sixteen days in a three-by-nine-foot cell, blindfolded and continually abused. He came out more determined than ever. The Committee of Mothers of the Disappeared continue their public denunciations in spite of threats, arrests, beatings and killings. 'The worse the repression, the braver the people get,' said a member of the base communities.

Tonia doesn't use the word 'option' any longer: 'It is an integration, an insertion, as it were: it is to feel as the people feel, to run the same risks. Archbishop Romero is a good example: he absorbed what it really means to be poor. He used to say "We must feel with the church," and he thought that to feel with the church was to feel with the poor. I think the people remember this: he was not only *with*, — he *felt*.'

After a week I was saying to myself 'There is *no* option in El Salvador': it seemed to me that for the Christian, and especially for priests and sisters, solidarity with and commitment to the poor and oppressed was the only possible choice. I learnt, however, that for many there is another option: to withdraw into their safe, secure and traditional world, keeping their privileged position in large institutions, and justifying their choice by making an unreal distinction between spirituality and involvement. The division between those who hold very different concepts of what it means to be church in Latin America today extends into religious congregations.

The division was illustrated very clearly when refugees from the Mesa Grande camp in Honduras were returning, in groups, to El Salvador in 1987. Arriving at a town near the border, some of the new arrivals went to a convent to enquire about another group. The sister who came to the door said, 'Look, this doesn't concern us at all. Our concern is with things of the church.' Commenting on the incident, Tonia said, 'It's fear, more than anything. And also being somewhat disincarnated. If they were to go out and see, they would become more aware, but they're on the edge, apart... You can't be motivated by what you don't see.' The refugees themselves said, 'We don't want sisters who are busy with churches of stone, we want sisters who are with the church, because the church is us.'

A group of women catechists were asked what they expected of those in religious life. 'Well, you say you are religious,' they said, 'and you have given yourselves to God and to the people. So what we ask of you is that you be with the people, and that you denounce what is not of the kingdom, what destroys the kingdom, and then build a kingdom among us.'

Some of the Salvadorean sisters I spoke to had originally joined other congregations, but left when they realised that there was very little concern for the poor and very little understanding or tolerance of those who were so concerned.

'When I spoke of the poor to a nun, she was so trapped by the institution that she couldn't understand. Their Christ is a Christ of past history — they do not see him as present today.' Another sister quoted a nun as saying 'You are going to be religious, not pastoral workers.' Those who revered Archbishop Romero and wanted to accompany the people as he had done were labelled 'political' as opposed to 'religious' and 'spiritual'. 'But' said one, 'I am of the people and I want to be with them. I can't imagine a God who is not in the midst of the people. Any other god is a manufactured god.'

In one case, thirty-three members of one congregation left together. 'All of us who began to think differently had to leave. They spread calumnies about us, made our lives impossible, until one day we had to make up our minds and then we left. These congregations are well received by the institutional church, they don't question anything, they can get on peacefully with their teaching, go to the beach at weekends ...'

Some of the women who left continued to live in a lay community; others joined religious congregations who were closer to the people. The 1986 report of the Conference of Latin American Religious (CLAR) had this to say about young people joining the more traditional religious congregations:

> Some of the more traditional congregations are recruiting many young people from the rural areas surrounding cities where they have private schools. These vocations often come from traditional families whose religious background has not been touched by the spirit of Vatican II, Medellín and Puebla. These generous and sincere young people may have an idea of religious life which is overly influenced by the institution, the habit and the traditional image of the 'nun'. Superiors and formation personnel must be careful not to reinforce such an idea with a closed and traditional formation, but rather facilitate growth and renovation according to Vatican II, Medellín and Puebla. ... These young people must be given that type of formation which will permit them to be true leaders among their own people in their future apostolates. We must awaken in them a great desire to respond to the cry of the poor. We must resist any tendency in them to dissociate themselves from their people and become deaf to the problems of the poor and the demands of social justice. Certain characteristics of religious life today (convents, buildings, conveniences, isolation from the world of the poor) can paradoxically lead these young people to become indifferent to the total liberation of the poor. Entrance into religious life must not mean the opportunity for social and economic advancement, but rather a response to the gospel call to follow a Jesus who is poor in announcing the Good News to the poor.

Hearing the Word

There was a meeting for catechists in Guatajiagua, a small town near Gotera, one morning. In order to get there at ten o'clock, some of the catechists had had to set off on foot at 5.00 a.m.; one pregnant woman had walked down the mountain carrying a bag of oranges for the sisters. The men and women gathered in a meeting room, furnished with rickety wooden benches and a small table for the coffee and cakes that Anselma and Anne had brought, open on one side to let in a welcome breeze. People arrived slowly and the rest of us waited patiently — no European rush and agitation.

The discussion that day was based on a leaflet entitled 'Are there errors in the Bible?' Using Genesis 1 the various steps in creation were built up on a large sheet, showing that human beings were at the peak of God's creation.

'Not just some people, but all are made in his image,' said Anne. 'He didn't make some inferior to others, though some people are distorting God's plan by treating others as inferior. Woman, too, is made of flesh and bone, like man. She is not inferior.'

A necessary reminder in a society where *machismo* is still alive, and, indeed, in a church which is only just beginning to wake up to the fact that it has discriminated for centuries against half its members.

'God told us to take care of his creation, but some people are burning the crops and the hillsides and using up all the water. Water is very important; it is life, nothing can live without it. That is why it is used in baptism.'

'God gave his creation to everyone, but in El Salvador the land belongs only to a few.'

These catechists were learning to shed the light of God's word and his justice on their own situation. Before my eyes I saw the words of Puebla come alive: 'The base Christian communities embody the church's preferential love for the common people. In them their religiosity is expressed, valued, and purified; and they are given a concrete opportunity to share in the task of the church and to work committedly for the transformation of the world' (Puebla, Final Document, 643).

In the final prayers we thanked God for the opportunity of coming together to learn his Word, to understand it better, 'so that we can pass it on to others, so that God's kingdom may grow'.

Subversion

> If one understands the words of love that the church preaches ... one can also understand what is meant by accusations of 'sermons of subversion' or 'violence'. The church has not called upon the people to rise up against their brothers and sisters. But it has recalled two fundamental things. The first is what Medellín has to say about 'institutionalised violence'. When there really is present a situation of permanent, structured injustice, then the situation itself is violent. Secondly, the church is aware that anything said in that situation, even something undoubtedly prompted by love, will sound violent. But the church cannot refrain from speaking out' (Archbishop Oscar Romero, *Voice of the Voiceless*, New York, Orbis, 1985, London, CIIR, 1988, p. 77).

Archbishop Romero and the Jesuit Rutilio Grande are the best-known of many who supported the people and encouraged the popular organisations which sprang up in the 1970s when the persecution of the base ecclesial communities increased dramatically. The *Letter to the Churches* published by the Pastoral Centre of the Jesuit Central American University in San Salvador comments:

> From the gospel and with the gospel they committed themselves as pastors to the defence of the people. With it they not only proclaimed the faith and promoted justice, but they made such an impact on history that the sin of history did not tolerate them. They took a religious and pastoral stand against structural sin and structural sin murdered them. Their aim was not formally to change political structures, but to change the structures of sin (16-31 July 1988).

The experience of Tracy, a health worker in a rural area, is evidence that things have not changed in the 1980s:

> So many of the words and ideas that we use can be considered subversive: words like 'reality' and 'land' for instance. Helping refugees, getting food for them in an emergency, is considered to be a subversive activity. First aid is subversive because you could be teaching people how to bind up the wounds of guerrillas or how to remove bullets. In spite of this we must continue to preach a liberating message, and we do this by developing an alternative vocabulary. We cannot just wait with our arms folded until this war is over, but we

have to work out how to make our presence a stabilising influence while not putting the people in danger.

'Not sisters, but accomplished guerrillas'

Felipa described how she and another sister had tried to start a youth group in a nearby town.

> All during the meeting the soldiers were watching us closely to see what it was about. We invited them to take part in the songs, readings and group dynamics. Some of them joined in the singing. When we left, the soldiers called a meeting of the parents of the young people and told them not to let their children attend the meetings because we were subversives and would lead them into evil ways. They said, 'They pretend to be religious, but in fact they are accomplished guerrillas, and you are forbidden to send your children to these meetings.' About the same time the colonel went to visit the people in this area and told them that a guerrilla priest had been to a village with his wife and children and had given communion with bloodstained hands. Well, you can imagine what the young people were thinking of us by this time! When we arrived for the next meeting the young people were too afraid to come in, but eventually they came and I asked them if they would write out the fears that they felt in the group, and something about the way they thought I was going to lead them, and what hopes they had for the group. They wrote down all they felt and I explained the objectives that we had for the group. I said that I was not going to explain everything — they would have to investigate for themselves — but I certainly was not going to train them as subversives, or give them arms. The bible was the only 'arms' I had, but if speaking to them of the love of Jesus for us, and about the call God gives us, and the obligation we have to love our sisters and brothers: if for all that they call me subversive, then I admit it — I am.

Not only did this group continue to come to the meetings — they also brought others to join.

Pastoral work in the controlled zones

There are priests and sisters in the zones controlled by the FMLN in Chalatenango and Morazán, where there is a large civilian population. Their task is pastoral, making present the eucharist, the Christian community, the Word of God, the Jesus of the gospel, in the people's war. There are many among the combatants who came to the armed struggle through their Christian commitment, and who hunger for the Word of God and for contact with the church. The pastoral teams are there because they feel these people cannot be abandoned. Archbishop Rivera of San Salvador has commissioned priests to work in the war zones of Chalatenango, but those in Morazán work without the approval or support of their bishop. The military authorities seek to prevent visits to the controlled zones by church workers and recently asked church leaders to 'prevent the access of religious, lay people and priests to the areas of conflict'.

Pastoral work in these areas is extremely difficult. Many communities have no material for catechesis, no training or preparation of any kind for the catechists, no teachers, and therefore a high level of illiteracy. Churches have been destroyed by bombs and fear of bombings prevents people from coming to meetings; they are also afraid of coming to the celebration of the Word or the eucharist because the first question the soldiers ask when they arrive on a military operation is 'Who goes to the celebration or the mass?'

Some areas have not seen a priest for six years and there is a deep sense of having been abandoned by the church. The few priests, sisters and catechists who are there are anxious that the church recognise the work they are doing in the midst of so many difficulties, and that it guarantee their personal security, especially when the army enters the zone on military operations. They have invited the papal nuncio to visit them, and have asked the hierarchy to set up a system of visiting isolated parts in order to get to know their situation.

The papal nuncio was invited to visit communities in Gotera in 1986, but the night before he was due to go, the Ministry of Defence advised him against it, saying it was too dangerous. The disappointed people wondered where the danger could be coming from: 'From the guerrillas — in a town with an army garrison of 3000? From the military? But they issued the warning. So we must be the danger!'

A meeting in Copapayo with the communities there was also cancelled at the last minute, and for the same reason: the nuncio had been told by the military authorities that it was too dangerous. People from El Barrillo who had walked for two hours to get to the meeting were as disappointed as those in Copapayo, but the two groups consoled and encouraged each other.

'It is sad,' said Tonia, 'that the church authorities can get the permits but don't want to go, while we who work among the

people want to go but have great difficulty getting the permits.'
Happily, before I left I heard that the nuncio had accepted another invitation to visit Gotera.

In spite of all the difficulties, the pastoral presence in the controlled zones means that Christian life is continuing there, the faith is made incarnate in that situation; it is present in the struggle for justice, and a priestly presence with the people is assured.

4
Signs of Liberation

San Antonio Abad

When I returned to the capital from Gotera I stayed again with the Sisters of St Clare in their new house in San Antonio Abad, their old house having been destroyed in the 1986 earthquake. San Antonio Abad (St Anthony Abbot, the patron of the old parish church) is on the western outskirts of San Salvador, almost the nearest point of the capital to the San Salvador volcano. The neighbourhood became notorious in 1979 when a young priest, Octavio Ortiz, and four young men were killed by the army in the retreat house of El Despertar, not far from where the sisters are now living. In the 1970s the parish had been putting the Medellín guidelines into practice, the faith, hope and commitment of the people were growing, and soon 800 adults were taking an active part in the life of the community. It was the springtime of the Christian communities, they said, like the first success of Jesus in Galilee. El Despertar was used for meetings, and Octavio had been giving a leadership course when the army burst in and killed him and four of the young men following the course.

After the killings the community suffered dispersion, persecution and death: the fate of the authentic followers of Jesus. At a Holy Week liturgy in 1988 they remembered by name all those who had been killed in San Antonio Abad since 1979: exactly 401.

The sisters live off a badly paved road up a dirt track. Some houses have no piped water, rubbish is not collected and lies in piles by the side of the road. A few minutes away is the wealthy residential district of Colonia Escalón, with its beautiful mansions, brilliant flower gardens, well protected (from whom?) by massive gates and high walls topped with barbed wire or broken glass. It is not uncommon to see Cherokee Chiefs — large American estate cars notorious as the favourite vehicle of the death squads — gliding along its wide streets.

The sisters' house has a wire fence round it and a big double gate; it is roomy and airy inside and can stretch to accommodate many more than the half-dozen or so who are based there. The people in the neighbourhood, far from being envious of the house and its amenities, are delighted that one family among them at least has somewhere nice to live. Phyllis said, 'There is a great sense of communion with the people. We have a wall round the house and a front door, but we have people in the house almost twenty-four hours a day. They know we are here for them, and they come when they need us or when they just want to talk.'

I shared a room with Pat, an Irish sister who was visiting for some months; no one in the house had a bedroom to herself and there were sometimes three in a room and people sleeping in the living room. Folding beds are an essential part of the furniture. The community was fluid: two sisters are permanently there, others are on the move out to projects or off to Morazán to the camps for returned refugees.

Activities centred on the parish (catechetics, health care, literacy, sewing classes) and on the camps for displaced people and those returned from the Mesa Grande camp in Honduras.

> *Diary entry*
> Ash Wednesday in San Antonio Abad. Very hot evening. Church packed, two priests hearing confessions at the back; catechist in front inviting people to come to the microphone and comment on the meaning of Ash Wednesday. Several came up and spoke with assurance and feeling: the emphasis was on the need for change, on learning how to be church, how to forgive and love. Very alive and to the point. It was like liberation theology live! The whole thing lasted nearly three hours.

Forgiveness

I had heard many stories over the years of the capacity for forgiveness of the people of Nicaragua, Guatemala and El Salvador, and Phyllis told me of an experience she had had.

Anselma and I were going up to Cacaopera for a celebration of the Word, and when we got there the church was open, but no one was there. There was silence, tension in the air. Finally a catechist arrived and told us that soldiers had come in the night before and taken some people out and killed them. So we were going to leave, but another catechist said, 'Wait, the people will come'. About an hour later they started trickling in. The readings we had chosen didn't fit under the circumstances, so they started preparing the celebration, and it was all on the resurrection. I was really touched by the sharing, the readings. One of the mothers of one of the people killed prayed for the dead, and also for those who had killed them, that they would be forgiven, and that they would have the strength in their hearts to forgive themselves.

Phyllis went on, 'I thought, my God, if it had been me, and someone of my family had been killed, I'd be looking for vengeance, not praying for them twelve hours later.'

Diary entry for Monday 22 February 1988
The *paro* (transport stoppage called by the FMLN) began last night with lights going off. A lot of explosions and machine-gun fire during the night. Water cut off but on again this morning. The *paro* is expected to last for three days. They have been calling longer ones, but the people get fed up; they can just stand three days. I cooked kedgeree minus the fish plus fried onions and peppers for supper.

Tuesday 23rd. There were a lot of soldiers about yesterday evening. The explosions last night weren't so near. The soldiers were searching houses this afternoon. Had a long talk with Victoria about religious life. Victoria is very strong on being with the people, on not being so insistent on having daily mass and the Blessed Sacrament: how did we think the people prayed, she asked. Did we think we could keep God for ourselves? We felt that if the special things in religious life — silence, a certain regularity, etc. — didn't make us more open to the people, they were worthless. Tracy spoke about religious communities of the future: a nucleus of people committed for life, as religious are now, plus others, men, women, married, single. Religious today ought to be helping the laity. Religious life is changing direction and we ought to go along with this change.

Wednesday 24th. Paro still on. Armed police very evident.

Thursday 25th. Paro over. Set off for meetings after wiping floors with damp cloth and washing sheets. A lot of soldiers about still.

The women
Tonia spends much of her time driving around visiting the camps for returned refugees, and the places where the people are slowly returning to build up their lives again after the bombing of the early 1980s. She described to me how organised the people were, and how the women were sharing in the tasks of rebuilding and resettling their villages.

> The participation of women in the different tasks is important. They are on the organising committee of the camps, where they have a say in the discussions. They organise family groups; they feel that women are capable of doing everything the men do ... and more, very often. The men have come to realise that women have great resistance, and a big heart to love. It's great to see how little by little they are overcoming *machismo*.

Lucia came to the house one morning and told me how she and her mother had coped since her father and two of her brothers had been killed in 1980. Their house had been destroyed in the bombing, 55 people of the town had been massacred. For a long time Lucia and her mother and the youngest boy, aged 13 and now the head of the family, had wandered from place to place, desperately trying to earn enough money to live on. The boy used to go to the river at dawn to get sand and stones to sell. Eventually they learnt of a place where there was a building cooperative and they went there. Alicia, the mother, made and sold tortillas and Lucia worked with the 96 families who were building their houses. 'This was a big experience for me,' she said, 'I had never worked on a building site before, with spades and wheelbarrows. Then I began to get involved with the cooperative. We needed a health centre and I attended courses and learnt to give injections. Now I feel I can be of use.' She is now a leading member of her community, self-confident and proud to be able to contribute something.

'. . . and character produces hope'
Susan, a North American nurse training health promoters in a rural area, told me about the women she worked with.

> We are encouraging women to be health promoters — they are the natural healers in any family, any community, although the men, because they can read and write, usually end up being health

promoters. But a lot of women learned to read and write in the refugee camps — that time was not wasted and they've learnt a lot of skills. A group of them carried out an evaluation of their mental health. First, they listed all the factors that are stressful for them: how they were bombed, arrested, how the army wouldn't let the food through. They came out very high and very healthy in the evaluation, and with a real sense of their ability to make a difference in the communities if they get together and organise. One of the women said, 'The important thing is that we're committed. Of course we're scared, but it's not the fear that determines what we do, it's our commitment.'

For me personally [continued Susan] that has been a profound influence in terms of my own mental health, and what it means to be here. I see these women making choices that I know may result, if not now then eventually, in their deaths. Sometimes it's hard to watch people making that kind of decision, but when you know the strength of their commitment, and that when something does happen they don't fall apart... It's not like our First World expectations, that for a good Christian everything will go well, and if things don't, then there must be something wrong with us or with God. It's such a different way of having expectations about life. They expect pain and suffering from the decisions they make, and they get it, but it doesn't destroy them; it builds their character. They've been killed, harassed, bombed, but ... they're free. I'm always reminded of what Paul says in his Letter to the Romans: 'We rejoice in our sufferings, knowing that suffering produces endurance, and endurance produces character, and character produces hope ...' They have a hope that I need to learn from because it's certainly not part of First World theology. So I think that while politically there's a long way to go before this war's over, liberation is already taking place. It's not something that will happen all of a sudden at the end of the war — it's something that's growing and developing among the people now.

'Who is my neighbour?'

In answer to the question 'Who is my neighbour?' put to him by a teacher of the Law, Jesus told the story of the Good Samaritan (Luke 10:30-37). Susan told me this story:

A woman we work with came in one morning: the bus had been stopped at a checkpoint, the woman beside her didn't have up-to-date papers and the soldiers started giving her a hard time. She explained that because so many of the mayors' offices had been burnt down she hadn't been able to get her papers. So the soldier said, 'Well, what were you doing in that area — there were guerrillas there last night — you must have been helping them.' Then he looked round and asked, 'Can anyone vouch for this woman and confirm that what she is saying is true?' The woman who works for us said, 'Yes, I can vouch for her — I can guarantee that it's true.' She had never seen the woman in her life, but to me it's an example of the kingdom of God. At that moment that woman did become her friend: she saw a person in need and she responded, and she wasn't lying when she said 'This woman's my friend.' And the soldier let the other woman go. That is Christian living at its most basic. These women have found the spirit of liberation. People like that, who can't be controlled by fear, are liberated.

The beginning of the end of *machismo*?

Jon Sobrino in a recent interview commented on the structural oppression of women in Latin American society:

> I see machismo in different social classes and in various forms; an unequal burden of work among men and women, often worse rewarded in the woman than in the man, heavier and more demanding for the woman, but less appreciated socially because it is considered normal. And I see too that the women have to assume responsibilities for the children that they cannot neglect socially, nor should they do so morally, but which men can disregard and neglect much more easily. And the women have very much less power to change society and the realities and social attitudes which affect them.

He goes on to say that women as well as men are responsible for the continuation of this state of affairs, since some of them seem to have accepted *machismo*, and even allow themselves to be dominated by the men in some things so that they can be dominant in others.

These issues were discussed at a meeting for married couples in Lolotiquillo, a small town not far from Gotera. After bumping over a badly potholed road in our truck, Anselma and I arrived early and while we waited for the couples we walked through the dusty street in the burning sun to a small 'shop' where we bought cold drinks and sat for a while in the welcome shade. It always amazed me that ice was available in these small places — wonderfully refreshing in the heat and dust.

More couples had reached the meeting place when we returned, and were sitting round on the low wall of a sort of summer-house roofed with palm leaves beautifully shaped and rising to a point. Children ran in and out; some of the men practised on the guitar.

The theme of the day was the problems of married life. These men and women were learning to value their relationship. Four groups acted out different styles of married life, with a good deal of merriment: the considerate husband, the united and harmonious family, the drunk, the lazy wife. Perceptive comments followed:

> 'The man expects the wife always to have his meals ready on time.'
>
> 'The woman can be too docile.'
>
> 'But if you let your wife have some independence, she'll end up dominating you.'
>
> 'The man can take advantage of a humble woman to lord it over her.'
>
> 'How good if a man would show concern for his wife and take care of her when she is tired or ill!'
>
> 'Instead of the wife giving her husband his medicine with a rough remark, how much better if she did it gently and lovingly!'

There was a very sensitive understanding of the effects of *machismo* on both men and women, and a real desire to develop a more equal relationship. Reflection on the bible had been important in their married lives; as one woman put it, 'Before my husband heard the Word of God, my life was very difficult.'

This group, like many others I met, knew from experience that the Word of God has power to change, and that the place for hearing the Word is the community.

'Not classic nuns'

In *Death and Life in Morazán* Fr Rogelio Ponceele, writing about the early days of the communities in Zacamil, mentions a group of women — 'half nuns, something special, not classic nuns, something else' — who had gone through a process of conversion and had committed themselves to the people, forming a new kind of religious community.

Silvia Arriola was one of the early members of this group, which now numbers eleven in El Salvador, and is spreading to other Latin American countries: Brazil, Nicaragua and Costa Rica. A portrait of Silvia hangs on the living-room wall, and she is remembered in the calendar of the Martyrs of the base communities: 'For several years she was secretary to Archbishop Romero, before whom she pronounced her religious vows. She left the religious congregation she had first joined to begin a new experience of Christian community at the service of the poorest. Always seeking to do the will of God, she left everything to take up the pastoral work of accompanying the people and was killed on 17 January 1981.' Silvia was nursing the wounded in a zone controlled by the FMLN when an attack by the army cost her her life.

I stayed in the Little Community's house in San Salvador and shared their life for a couple of days. Their simple life style and the way they work appeals to young women: those who ask to join them meet regularly for study and discussion, though there is no specific training programme. After a year with the community, if a young woman wishes to join and is accepted, she prepares to make vows of poverty, chastity and obedience. Some of those I met, however, had said they were not ready to make a public commitment. Their pastoral work with the base communities is central, and they recognise the necessity for prayer and study if this is to continue to be fruitful. Each morning they meet for an hour's reflection on the gospel in their small chapel, and one day a week is given to study.

One morning at the breakfast table I wondered aloud why they had decided to form a religious community rather than remain actively involved in the church as lay women. Carmen Elena answered me:

> Although we are not legally a religious congregation — we have no documents or rules, no relationship with the archdiocese here or with Rome — we do believe in the religious life. We believe in a religious life which brings life to others; we think that the religious life can be an answer for many young women, many new desires, which could renew the church. We believe in the church and feel we are called to contribute to the church and to serve the church by living as consecrated women.

The originality of this group lies in its close links with the base ecclesial communities from which it sprang.

> We think that the Christian base communities have the right to have, within the richness of their life, a form of religious life proper to them. But the institutional life is not for us. We share in the religious life in union with the other sisters here and with the institutional church, but through the legitimacy that service gives in the church.

Ana added:

> Our community aims to renew the church a little and show how it is possible in this way to live a community life, to live like sisters, without a hierarchy. We saw the value of the religious life as a way of consecration to the God manifested in the communities, in the suffering people, and we saw that it was possible to live the consecrated life within the base communities, among the people, as a response to them. The religious life would have no meaning if it were not a response to the people.

On Saturday afternoon I accompanied a group of women 'missionaries' who were visiting the shacks nearby and explaining the Sunday mass readings to the people. 'There is bad news for our people today, so we take them the good news of our friendship and concern', said Noemi. Later, a meeting of catechists discussed strategy as they prepared to evangelise new groups during Lent. As in the early days of the base communities, house visits came first; then the people would be invited to take part in the Via Crucis, the Way of the Cross, since it was the first week in Lent. Noemi emphasised the importance of making the Via Crucis accord with their own lives, and not letting it just be a devotional exercise. 'We are living a Via Crucis in El Salvador today; we must pray it with our life in our hands.'

El Paraíso Cooperative
Sitting in Felicita's hut, drinking a *fresco* and eating homemade cake, I listened to her and to Lidia describe the beginnings of the cooperative, where 60 families, about 300 people, now live. The initiative had come from a priest and became a real community venture, with everyone helping.

'A project like this' said Lidia, 'based on socialist principles, has many problems in El Salvador. The military are watching us day and night. We are tired of seeing so much blood, so many dead. The death squads are at work again; one, called "The White Hand", leaves the mark of a white hand on doors as a death threat.'

Padre Pedro had brought a new method, a new way of reading the gospel. He was with the people, celebrated the eucharist in different houses, helped couples to be reconciled. The people began to get interested as they saw a different church from the traditional one 'centred on the rites'.

The church that now began to emerge studied the documents of Vatican II, Medellín and Puebla. 'There we discovered,' continued Lidia, 'that all lay people are called to be missionaries, to spread God's word. Little by little we became more committed and began to draw others in. There are a lot of missionaries here, still working; we don't want to lose the spirit we have here.' The priest had wanted the community to be a sign that 'the poor can unite and organise to achieve their objectives.' He had thanked them for helping him to rediscover his faith, and when the persecution obliged him to return to Europe, the Salvadorean experience enabled him to begin building communities there.

Lidia spoke of Archbishop Romero as the pastor who had done most to help them 'stand up'.

> He was a true prophet; we have missed him. We need him. His voice opened many hearts; his echo was heard all over the country. In his homilies he denounced what was happening. The true prophets are like that — they announce the good news, but they denounce at the same time. He was impartial, he told the truth. It hurt him to say what he did. We compare him with Jesus: they couldn't silence him with threats, or buy him off. Archbishop Romero said that as long as the repression lasted he would not sit down with the government. And he kept his word.

Lidia repeated what I heard from many others, 'The greater the repression, the braver people become.'

The women spoke a little about unemployment and the high cost of living. 'This is democracy with hunger,' said Lidia. Black beans, the staple diet, had risen four times in price since the previous year. 'What about meat?' I asked. They laughed': 'Nine colones a kilo (just under US$2).' A group had asked the priest at the beginning of Lent what fasting was. 'How often have you eaten meat this year?' he asked. 'Never, Father.' 'Then you have been fasting.' 'Oh, thank you, Father. We only wondered what it was.' Sitting in Felicita's poor hut, clean but poorly furnished, these women, who had had very little education, were able to discuss their social and political situation, describe the development of the community and talk about their understanding of what it means to be church in El Salvador today. As someone remarked, 'There are things that God reveals to the humblest. There are educated people who do not understand.'

5
Signs of hope

'Our desert is in El Salvador'
The gospel reading for the first Sunday in Lent was the temptation of Jesus in the desert — a theme that meant much to the priest who celebrated the eucharist in the church in Zacamil. He himself had been arrested by the military and knew fear and how faith could be shaken. Among those who shared their reflections on the story of the temptation of Jesus was a woman who came up, very timidly, at the end. 'We women,' she said, 'have to be clear that we have a lot of responsibility in the Christian life. Our desert is in El Salvador, now. I too am frightened, but the Lord is with us. We all know that Christianity is not for the other world but for the here and now. We have to unite and share our faith.' She was warmly applauded and returned to her seat obviously encouraged and pleased.

After the mass I spoke to Alejandro Ortiz, the father of Octavio Ortiz, who was murdered in El Despertar in 1979. Alejandro had lost three other sons and his wife was a refugee in another country. There was no bitterness in his face, which reflected tranquillity and peace, the fruits of a truly Christian forgiveness.

Dolores was a member of the widows' group. Her husband had been killed in 1980; she had also lost a son of 16 and two brothers in the repression. Two other sons had been captured by the army but had escaped and gone to the mountains to join the FMLN. Dolores had herself been detained. 'And just for being Christian' she said.

Elsa's daughter had been blown up by a mine; her son had had his eyes gouged out and was then shot to pieces. Now the soldiers were looking for Elsa herself. 'If you are doing church work, they look for a way to destroy you.'

In spite of what they had gone through, these women were calm, committed and ready to talk about their faith.

> 'We don't believe in death without resurrection.'
> 'You carry the pain of your loss always with you.'
> 'They are dismembering Jesus — God is incarnate in us.'
> 'We don't cry with our eyes, we cry with our hearts.'
> 'Compassion, not pity. You pity a dog.'
> 'We carry on.'

On the church wall behind us were posters: 'The gospel of peace is a fight to the death for life.' And some words from Silvia Arriola's vows: 'In a society whose ideals are power, possession and pleasure, I pray that I may be a sign of what it really means to love.'

Basic Ecclesial Communities

In 1969 a group of European priests began gathering people together and planting hope in the midst of the poverty and despair of the slums of San Salvador: those ravines running like festering wounds across the capital, sometimes just across the road from elegant residential areas. Over the next ten years the communities grew, the people began to develop a sense of their worth and potential, and their lives began to change.

> It was a great miracle to see a scattered people come together again. We were beginning to be one people. Everywhere little groups were forming, becoming communities. The gospel was the book from which the communities learned who they were, and from which they learned the reality of the situation in which they lived' (*Faith of a People*, New York, Orbis Books, London, CIIR, Melbourne, Dove Communications, 1986).

After the first euphoria and the first surge of success, the criticism and the questions began, first from those sectors of the church surprised by the new-found confidence and the organisation of the people, who, in their turn, were none too complimentary about the religion they had been taught. Then the state authorities denounced the communities as hotbeds of communism and subversion. By the end of the 1970s the persecution had become so severe that the priests were obliged to leave the capital. On 5 November 1980 their house in Zacamil was blown up.

Zacamil, a comparatively well-off neighbourhood on the west of the capital, has large blocks of flats cheek by jowl with a sprawl of makeshift shacks sheltering the victims of the 1986 earthquake. Very little of the aid which poured into El Salvador after the earthquake reached the poor, whose flimsy shacks had been the first to collapse. The people on this piece of land had even been threatened with eviction unless they paid for their 'dwellings', cardboard and corrugated iron.

Meme, a mild-spoken man in his early fifties, has been in the communities since the beginning, and sitting in the large shed which does duty as a church (built on the site of the priests' house), he told me about them one afternoon.

> We began in our communities in 1969 by realising, through our group reflections, that in fact the church did not exist, and it was precisely this which motivated this group of priests to try to bring this church into existence, before worrying about a building. We have now had the communities for 19 years and we still have no church building; we have this place, where we are now, and other places for meetings and the liturgy, but no formal church. We are conscious that the church is not a building — it is all the baptised, who know they have a mission to accomplish. We have understood, in the base communities, that we are a new way of being church. Traditionally, the Catholic Church has limited itself to dispensing the sacraments, without much in the way of gospel teaching and reflection with the people. Today this is the great task of our communities — to evangelise, but to evangelise from people's lives.

Visits come first, then small groups are formed for discussion and reflection on the people's problems. 'After discussing, we try to throw light on these problems and on our responsibility in the light of the gospel. That is how our communities work.'

The persecution began in the mid 'seventies and was first aimed at selected leaders. Many foreign priests were expelled.

Salvadorean priests and members of the communities were persecuted and over those years 600 members of the Zacamil communities were murdered.

> 'In all this' continued Meme, 'the communities dispersed. Meetings were not possible; we had to resort to another way of evangelising and

holding meetings. But all that was not enough to kill our spirit — and here we still are! We see that it is the Spirit of Christ which is accompanying the people on their pilgrimage through this world, and it is this same Spirit which gives us life.'

Later that day I visited the spot where Herbert Anaya, head of the independent Human Rights Commission of El Salvador, had been shot dead in October 1987 as he was taking his children to school. A simple cross marks the place on the pavement, outside a row of houses, where they gunned him down. His widow, Mirna, spoke characteristic words of forgiveness at his funeral in the cathedral. 'I do not demand vengeance on those who butchered my husband. ... I want to say to them that my husband never hated them. I want to say that my husband, if he could be with us now, would say that he forgave them.'

The faith of the people

> The faith of the people is different from that of some sectors of the church, the hierarchy — the people believe in a God of life. They have not lost their faith, as they are accused of having done. Their attitudes are different from those who are on the side of the powerful. The people want to speak the truth — they make an option for the truth, then they put their truth to the test of the gospel. They ask 'What is God's will' — there is nothing of their own interest. They disturb the system, so they are a nuisance. They are on the side of the gospel of the will of God and of the truth. The person who reads the bible has to be free of self-interest, and not manipulate the Word (A Salvadorean sister).

Prayer

> There are two kinds of prayer: there's the prayer of the moment, when something happens, like the day of the earthquake when we just stood in the middle of the street and started praying with the people. Then there's the prayer that's prepared. They each have their own flavour, but the underlying truth is: there's a God that's present (Phyllis).
>
> Prayer is completely different here in El Salvador. When I read the passion of Christ in the gospel I see Juan, Ramón, Bartola — so many who have gone through their own passion. It's not 2000 years ago, it's here and now. The book of Revelation too has tremendous meaning

for us: a wartime context, people writing letters to each other in code ... (Anne).

Prayer is something basic in my Christian experience — it underlies all my needs. Often I feel discouraged and I turn to prayer out of my own experience and needs. It is marvellous to have a personal, solitary contact with God, it is what strengthens me and helps me to go on growing in my faith, with God in whom I believe and with the poorest, who are today clamouring for our help, for our outstretched hand; to be able to accompany the people... (Aida).

The liturgies here are lived — people take part — they're real. If we need rain, we pray for rain; if someone's just been killed, we pray for them; if there's a fight in the community we pray about that. Whatever is going on in the community is touched and prayed for. God is a God who walks with us; he doesn't want a lot of formalised prayers, he wants us to talk to him and have a relationship with him. (Phyllis).

I couldn't live all this activity and have this strength unless there was something urging me on. I just couldn't go on. But I feel the strength that comes from prayer, and prayer very often has to be a response to a situation (Tonia).

A celebrant of the Word speaking about Mary, the mother of Jesus:

'How do you see her in the church?'
'Humble and simple.'
'Are you sure that she is always portrayed humble and simple?'
'No, she has painted lips.'
'She has an expensive dress.'
'Have you ever seen Mary with a dress like yours?'

Everyone then began commenting on Mary's qualities, bringing out what she must really have been like.

Anselma: 'Reading the Bible is so different in El Salvador: the words just jump out of the page at you — it is so close to the situation the people are living.'

The psalms we said at morning prayer might have been spoken by the people who came to the house:

Psalm 56
Have mercy on me, God, foes crush me; they fight me all day long and oppress me. My foes crush me all day long, for many fight proudly

against me. When I fear, I will trust in you.
Psalm 26
O Lord, I love the house where you dwell, the place where your glory abides. Do not sweep me away with sinners, nor my life with bloodthirsty people in whose hands are evil plots, whose right hands are filled with gold.
Psalm 117
I called to the Lord in my distress; he answered and freed me. The Lord is at my side; I do not fear. What can mortals do against me? The Lord is at my side as my helper; I shall look down on my foes.

El Paisnal church — a danger zone

There is a spot by the side of the road between Aguilares and El Paisnal which could easily be passed by — the three crosses planted there are so small and simple. The one in the middle has a plaque with the words: 'Rutilio Grande SJ, Martyr, 12 March 1977'. The other two bear the names of the old man and the boy who were killed with him: Manuel Solórzano and Nelson Rutilio Lemus. At this holy spot a group of Jesuits and others gathered on Thursday 3 March 1988. Someone had brought out a new plaque for Rutilio's cross, which was always being removed by persons unknown, and fixed it on while we watched. As he worked, another car drew up and a short man in clerical black got out: the Father General of the Jesuits, Peter-Hans Kolvenbach, on his first visit to El Salvador. He listened attentively to an account of how Rutilio and his two companions had been gunned down in their pickup when they were on their way to El Paisnal for the eucharist. We said an Our Father, a Hail Mary, a prayer for Rutilio and his companions, then quickly got into the cars and drove on to El Paisnal since even today, eleven years later, it is dangerous to show that you remember what happened to Rutilio. It was a moving moment but quite undramatic: violent death is an ever-present reality in El Salvador and needs no dramatisation.

The little church in El Paisnal had been cleaned up for the occasion and the key had to be fetched from the nearby town of Aguilares, since El Paisnal has been almost abandoned because of the repression and the war. Coloured lights flickered on and off round a statue on the back wall, a few people came and placed candles and flowers on the three graves before the altar, and the church filled up with people, many of whom had come from the capital to take part in this historic eucharist. About 80 Jesuits from all over Central America and the northern countries of South America were present, gathered round the altar in white albs and brightly embroidered stoles. In his homily Father Kolvenbach spoke of 'This great priest and Jesuit, our brother and the brother of all men and women, especially of the poorest, Rutilio Grande' and of his 'companions in martyrdom'. His words were a strong response to those who still today publish calumnies about Rutilio. At the end of the mass a group sang a song about Rutilio — it was the Christian community acknowledging its debt to its martyrs and expressing its solidarity with them in faith, hope and love.

As we got into the cars for the journey back to the capital, an old woman said, 'I hope nothing will happen to you on the way.' In fact, the army had been conspicuous by its absence — had they been warned to keep out of the way because a Jesuit VIP was visiting? An article in a Jesuit publication says of El Paisnal church: 'A meeting place before, the church is now a danger zone: Rutilio is buried there.'

Martyrdom

Martyrdom is still a possibility that has to be reckoned with in El Salvador. Phyllis told me how in their community they were careful not to prolong quarrels:

> Here, if you have a fight with someone, you try to work it out quickly, because you don't have the energy to maintain it, but also you never know if you're going to see the person again once they walk out of the door. We are living in the midst of a civil war. It's not something really conscious, but I remember one day we had a community meeting and we decided to sit down and talk about martyrdom and what it meant, and look at it in a biblical sense, and look for the strength to continue facing it, because it was an unspoken reality that we were living with. So you tend not to take each other so much for granted.

The Basic Ecclesial Communities of El Salvador bring out a calendar with, for each month, a list of their members killed by the army or the security forces, under the heading: 'They gave their lives for the gospel.' Here are some examples.

> May 11, Fr Alfonso Navarro. In the agony of his martyrdom, Fr Alfonso, parish priest of the Colonia Miramonte, said, 'I die because I preached the gospel. I know who my murderers are. Let them know that I forgive them.' +1977.

Such was the persecution of the church, and the fear engendered by it, that some families forced their children to leave home because they refused to give up their work as catechists. Gladis was one of these:

> July 17, Gladis Elizabeth Carpio Sánchez and sixteen fellow catechists, assassinated by shooting and stabbing in El Sauce, San Martín, Department of San Salvador. Since the age of 13 when she made her first communion, Gladis worked as a catechist. When, out of fear, some parents expelled their children who were catechists from their houses, since they would not abandon the work of the church, Gladis used to prepare food and take it to them. One day when they were gathered in a house, the military surrounded the area, together with security forces, and they murdered them. Gladis was 17. +1980.

In fidelity to the opening words of *Gaudium et Spes*, the Salvadorean church has made its own the anguish and hopes of others, especially the poor and oppressed. As a result it has suffered the same fate as the poor, which it defines in theological terms as persecution. Perhaps the most moving reflection on this aspect of the church's life is that of Archbishop Romero, in his address in Louvain in 1980:

> It is an indisputable fact that... our church has been persecuted. But it is important to note why it has been persecuted. Not any and every priest has been persecuted, not any and every institution has been attacked. That part of the church has been attacked and persecuted that put iself on the side of the people and went to the people's defense... Persecution has been occasioned by the defense of the poor. It amounts to nothing other than the church's taking upon itself the lot of the poor. Real persecution has been directed against the poor, the body of Christ in history today... And for that reason when the church has organized and united itself around the hopes and anxieties of the poor it has incurred the same fate as that of Jesus and of the poor: persecution (*Voice of the Voiceless*, New York, Orbis Books, 1985, London, CIIR, 1988, p.182).

It is not the persecution of the church which causes pain, but the continued suffering of the people. The hope is not just that peace may return to the church, but that peace and justice may return for the people.

Liberation is taking place

Visitors to El Salvador are struck by this: that at the base, among the poorest, the displaced, the refugees and in the zones controlled by the FMLN, the new society is already in the making, and the ideals of selflessness, sharing and simple living are becoming part of its fabric. Here are some comments, made by both visitors and people living in the country:

> People living in El Salvador are already living the kind of life they want after the war. Not only longing for it, but living it. We should begin now, in small ways, to live our ideals (A sister of Charles de Foucauld, on a visit from Spain).
>
> I feel it's a great privilege being here with the people, sharing in their search and their struggle: we're in a church that's alive. They're trying to understand what God wants for them; not a God that's put on a pedestal, but a God that lives and walks along with them. He's a God that is very real in the middle of our search for a new society, for a change in the structures... (A North American sister).
>
> These people who have returned from the refugee camp in Honduras want to be self-sufficient, to be able to face life as a community; they never think in terms of 'each one for himself'... Face life together, go hungry together, if they have something, share it with everyone. A nation is being built up in these places — a people that will inspire us all to find a new meaning to life, a new strength of faith and hope (A Salvadorean sister).
>
> Now, at this moment, life in the controlled zones is as beautiful as you can imagine. In the midst of everything you feel happy, entertained; no disagreements among us, we live like brothers. There's a lot of fellowship and companionship among us. In an ordinary army those who command are apart, so that you can't go up to them and say what you think, because that would be lacking in respect. But with us there is always respect with an officer, but more sincerely. Orders are given affectionately so they gain one's friendship and respect, and in turn one tries not to offend them. We are very united, like a family. There is *machismo* in a capitalist army, but there shouldn't be in a revolutionary army. We are in a struggle for liberation and we have first to liberate ourselves from all our mistakes, from our bad ways of living. We have to liberate ourselves before we can liberate the people (A wounded guerrilla, now out of the fighting).

A new diocese and a new bishop

Tonia and I left the house in San Antonio Abad at 7.00 a.m. to go to Chalatenango for the ordination of Eduardo Alas as the first bishop of the new diocese of Chalatenango. It was Saturday 27 February. We picked up Peter O'Neill at the Franciscan house and on the way took on board as many as we could from the groups waiting hopefully at the roadside. It seemed that everyone was on the way to Chalatenango and as we got nearer banners strung across the road announced 'Welcome to the new diocese of Chalatenango' and 'Welcome to Mgr Eduardo Alas, new bishop of Chalatenango.' Even in the midst of war, it seemed, the people still had the will and the energy and the creativeness to make the most of a celebration.

Chalatenango was packed with people and vehicles when we got there, and very hot. Processions from other places were arriving, each with its own banner: the group from Arcatao had walked 32 kilometres and their banner read: 'I will visit my sheep and gather them from the places where they have been scattered' — a quotation from Ezekiel with even more meaning in a region where so many have been displaced. The streets were strung with bunting and full of people in their Sunday best, the men with big straw hats, the women with newspapers or towels covering their heads.

A simple altar, roofed with palms, had been placed in the square beside the church. A huge poster of Archbishop Romero bore his words: 'I am with my people.' There were soldiers everywhere, even a machine-gun emplacement in the church tower, which I was told was a permanent feature. The courageous Mothers of the Disappeared had been threatened with excommunication when they occupied the cathedral to draw attention to the fate of their relatives, while armed soldiers were allowed to occupy a church tower, even during a service.

The ceremony of ordination lasted three hours, in the burning sun, and the crowds stayed to the end. Later, the newsletter of the Pastoral Centre of the Central American University commented on the ceremony and noted how the official ecclesial event was clearly distinct from the people's religious event:

> Nearly everything took place on the altar while the people looked on. For them much of the language, of the explanations and of the homily was far too abstract. There was a good deal about what a bishop is,

but hardly any mention of the reality of the new diocese of Chalatenango, or of the people of God in this diocese, the suffering people of Chalatenango, or of what a bishop should be like in such situations.

Nevertheless, the people made their contribution to the official ceremony by praying, singing, clapping, waving their banners — bringing their suffering presence with joy into the liturgy of salvation. They even went so far as to let off fireworks during the address of the new bishop — a custom which, I was told, it is difficult to restrain! At least they cannot be accused of passive attendance. As the newsletter's account put it, 'Before the church made an option for the poor, the poor made an option for the church.'

Celebrating the eucharist in Calle Real

On my last Sunday in El Salvador a Jesuit friend took me to the Calle Real camp for displaced people about 10kms north of the capital. I had visited Calle Real in 1986, shortly after it was set up by the archdiocese of San Salvador to receive people displaced by the war and as a centre for people from rural areas requiring medical treatment. Two years later the camp was still full, this time with the addition of a number of wounded FMLN combatants, who were being given shelter and medical attention there under the protection of the Catholic Church and the International Committee of the Red Cross. Medical facilities for the guerrillas are rudimentary in the controlled zones, and often attacked by the army, in violation of the Geneva Convention.

The atmosphere in the camp that Sunday was tense. On Saturday 16 January heavily armed troops had entered the camp, searched it for arms, and identified 22 people whom they wanted to take away. The intervention of Mgr Ricardo Urioste, the vicar general of the archdiocese of San Salvador, and Fr Octavio Cruz led to the soldiers leaving without the 22 but saying they would return. The next day, Sunday, soldiers positioned round the camp fired sporadically all day, until at 9.20 p.m. firing began in earnest and continued for about an hour and a half.

After this incident a military checkpoint was set up outside the camp and all arrivals had to show their papers before being allowed to continue. It seemed to me outrageous that a camp established by the church could be attacked, and that the military were then allowed to monitor all access.

Before the mass we chatted to the people, who were still very nervous. Some of the children showed me their drawings, and one small boy, Jermán, gave me his drawing of an army helicopter with armed soldiers inside — a very real part of his world. Another little fellow with great courtesy asked my name, my father's name, my mother's name, and sent them his greetings. His mother had been killed but his father was with him in the camp.

The mass took place under the shade of a tree, with a few benches around for older people or nursing mothers. Though it was Lent, we sang the Gloria, because, as Padre Jon said, 'We Christians aren't sad.' The response to the psalm was 'I will walk in the presence of the Lord in the land of the living', and at the Peace we sang 'Peace, we want peace; freedom among us all.'

In his homily on the story of Abraham being asked to sacrifice his son Isaac, Padre Jon commented:

> God was asking something very hard of Abraham to test his faith. What is God asking of us? Very difficult things: he is asking us to keep together; or perhaps to go to the celebration of the Word when we are quite comfortable in our hammocks; or to see that the children go to their doctrine class; or to respect and care for one another.

The emphasis was on building community, on sharing in very simple ways, like not taking too big a spoonful of sugar.

> We are from different places but it's the same struggle, so we mustn't make differences between ourselves. We must know how to help each other, we must teach our children how to live as brothers and sisters. Let's all work together. I don't know if you agree?'

'Yes, Father, you're right!' they chorused. The priest responded with a memorable image:

> We must give the gospel little feet, so as to spread the Word. Archbishop Romero used to tell us to proclaim the Word. We are the little feet of the gospel.

Some of the people then spoke, encouraging the others to take the step of moving out of the camp and back to their places of origin: a frightening prospect for many, but a necessary move if they are ever to get back to normal living.

'Christ may be inviting us to another place,' said one man, 'but if we don't want to make the sacrifice we can say, with Peter in the gospel, "We're all right here, let's build ourselves huts here." But we must ask where we can serve best. Perhaps God is asking us to leave the little we have here.'

The petitions were read out from slips of paper the people had put on the altar:

> Father, I want you to please pray for these people who died in a massacre on 26 February 1982 in Guazapa: my parents, brothers and brothers-in-law and my father-in-law.
>
> Father, I want you to please pray for my brother José, his two daughters and 13 grandchildren, who died with him on 27 February 1982 in a massacre in Guazapa.
>
> For those who have economic and political responsibilities, that they may make justice, understanding and peace reign.
>
> For our brother Eduardo Alas Alfaro, priest, who yesterday, Saturday 27 February 1988, was ordained bishop in Chalatenango. That the sacrifice and joy of many Christians may be the hope of their new bishop, and that the Holy Spirit may give him strength to build, sanctify and govern the church.
>
> For those who are here united, that in this time of Lent we may truly decide to live as new men and women in every situation.
>
> Lord Jesus, your transfiguration is reflected in so many suffering faces, in the faces of so many prisoners who are inhumanly ill-treated, in the committed Christians tortured for their faith, in the sad faces of abandoned old people, in the faces of so many malnourished and orphan children. For those who are disfigured by blows, hunger, misery, exploitation and torture, let us pray to the Lord.
>
> Let us pray that, announcing the joy of the gospel, the power of Christ risen may grow everywhere.

A woman standing next to me told me that, because she had survived the massacres and bombing of Guazapa, one of the priests had jokingly called her 'the bad weed that doesn't burn'. Niña Teya had herself been detained by the army:

> In Lent we think of Jesus and what he suffered: blows, spitting. They did these things to me too and I thought of Jesus while they were doing them. They asked me many things but I wasn't going to tell them.

'You can do what you like to me', I said. I was eleven days without food, but I had faith in God. He died to show us how to live. He rose to give us hope.

Conclusion

Before I went to El Salvador to gather material for this book, a colleague advised, 'Don't go armed with set questions. They will be European questions and not relevant in El Salvador.' When I arrived, a Jesuit friend said, 'Let the people and their experiences speak in your book. Not too many of your own reflections.'

Remembering this advice, I have tried to let the people and the events I have recorded speak for themselves. The richness of the experience needs no embroidering by me: I could only share it for a short time with a great feeling of awe and gratitude, and then try to communicate it in all its simplicity.

Nevertheless there are some aspects I would like to highlight as having a message for us in our very different world. The committed church in El Salvador, indeed, in Latin America as a whole, is good news for the church in Europe. The challenge of Vatican II has been taken up and developed: a new way of being church, a new understanding of Christian commitment and Christian presence in the world, is being worked out. This committed church is one in which religious life is integrated into the life of the local church in a way which it often is not in Europe. The profession of Elvia and Juana in Cacaopera was part of the life of the local parish: the people knew what they wanted of the sisters, and the sisters saw their consecration as religious in terms of response to the people. By committing themselves to a particular religious congregation, Elvia and Juana were binding themselves more closely to the Christian community, not separating themselves from it. There is a message here which religious congregations in Europe must take to heart and ponder.

It is a church of the people — a priestly and prophetic people — incarnated in the historical reality of El Salvador today. What touches the country touches the church: the political, the social and the ecclesial are interwoven, and for many Christians there is no watertight religious compartment, no standing on the edge, apart, looking on and making 'spiritual' or 'religious' judgments on events without feeling in any way responsible for what is happening. Sadly, as some incidents in this book show, not all sections of the Salvadorean church share this commitment. Many, however, have had to make difficult choices — choices which are not just for politics or for the struggle, but for the kingdom of God and the primacy of his will, and against everything which is contrary to these.

The sisters I met and the people they serve have made their choice and accepted the consequences. Commitment to the transformation of the world lies at the heart of their choice, and it confronts all Christians with the question whether caring for the victims of society is the only, or the most appropriate, form of ministry. They show us a situation in which doing only that can be an evasion. They help us to see how in the life and practice of the Old Testament prophets and of Jesus denunciation of oppressive systems and liberating action on behalf of those suffering under them are integral to the proclamation of the Good News. It was witness like theirs which led the 1971 synod of bishops to declare formally: 'Action on behalf of justice and participation in the transformation of the world fully appear to us as a constitutive dimension of the preaching of the gospel or, in other words, of the church's mission for the redemption of the human race and its liberation from every oppressive situation.'

Christians in El Salvador have taken the whole of Mary's Magnificat to heart, not just the first part. For them, recognition of and gratitude for the power of God working in each individual leads logically to action: turning unjust systems upside down in the spirit of the Magnificat. For them the choice is between a church which upholds the status quo, saying nothing that could be considered a threat to it, anxious to preserve its respectability, and a church which is incarnate in the world, with a mission to transform it according to the kingdom, no matter what the cost. This way of being church has consequences ranging from loss of respectability to loss of life. But the other way leads to an even greater loss.

My final word must be for the women of El Salvador. Through their active involvement in the changing political, social and ecclesial situation in their country, and in the struggle for justice, they are coming into their own. Centuries of male domination, a long history of enforced passivity, of being treated as objects, have not broken their spirit. Their role is changing, but their priorities are different from ours because their situation is different. I was made aware of my own European mindset when I presented a sister with a gift of an inclusive language edition of the psalms. She received it with puzzled politeness. This way of making a point is important for us, but in El Salvador, where life-or-death choices are daily occurrences, it is not a top priority. Their struggle for life, where death is very close for both women and men, is creating a new equality as they strive together to make a better world, free from fear.

More CIIR publications on faith and commitment in Central America

Available from bookshops or by mail from CIIR, 22 Coleman Fields, London N1 7AF, England

Letters from Nicaragua
John Medcalf
Foreword by Graham Greene

John Medcalf's letters bring to life on the page the brilliant colours of rural Nicaragua and the warmth of its people. His parishioners in Ox-ford, Monkey Face, Washtub and the Laurels have become flesh and blood for readers round the world. But his success in portraying this beauty only heightens the horror of the mangled limbs and charred timbers left behind by the Contra attacks the area endured from 1986 to 1988. Fr Medcalf turns the contrast into a moving plea for the right of Nicaragua to its own form of social and religious development.

'I have learnt all I know of the dangerous Contra central area from Father Medcalf's letters.'
Graham Greene

Hardback ISBN 1 85287 031 1 price £9.95
Paperback ISBN 1 85287 022 2 price £2.50

Faith of a People
The life of a Basic Christian Community in El Salvador, 1970-1980
Pablo Galdamez
Foreword by Jon Sobrino

The growth of basic Christian communities in Latin America has revolutionised the Roman Catholic Church. This book chronicles the development of one such community in El Salvador during the decade of turmoil, 1970-1980. Written by a member priest, **Faith of a People** recounts the experiences of a group of poor but faith-filled Christians — their crises and triumphs, hardships and rewards, pain and joy — as they sought a new definition of church and society. In the words of Jon Sobrino, 'The people and church of El Salvador emerged from anonymity and uttered a mighty word for the whole world to hear.'

'A passionate, poetic and highly concrete work.'
Library Journal

92pp 1986
ISBN 0 946848 48 3 price £5.95
Published in USA by Orbis Books
Published in Australia by Collins Dove

Prophets in Combat
The Nicaraguan Journal of Bishop Pedro Casaldáliga
Foreword by Leonardo Boff

Already famous for his defence of Brazilian peasants, Bishop Pedro Casaldáliga visited Nicaragua in 1986 to join Nicaragua's foreign minister, Fr. Miguel D'Escoto, in his 'gospel insurrection'. This book is the diary of his journey, in reports, meditations and peoms. It describes the courage and suffering of the Nicaraguan people, and argues that the cause of Nicaragua is crucial to the future of Latin America.

114pp 1987
ISBN 0 946848 94 7 price £4.95
Published in USA by Meyer Stone Books

Voice of the Voiceless
Archbishop Oscar Romero's Pastoral Letters and other Statements
Introductory essays by Jon Sobrino and Ignacio Martín-Baró

Throughout his life Archbishop Romero spoke out fearlessly against injustice and oppression. This book contains his four pastoral letters and other public statements in which he expounded the church's role in society and its duty to stand firm in the face of corruption and violence. There is a brief biography of Archbishop Romero, and a theological appreciation of his ministry.

'We have in him a concrete model of what a bishop, with a gospel faith, ought nowadays to be like, and an example of how important it is for a bishop to make that faith effective for liberation' (Jon Sobrino).

202pp indexed 1986
ISBN 0 946848 53 X price £8.95